BALANCE IT!

BALANCE IT!

by Howard E. Smith, Jr.
photographs by George Ancona

FOUR WINDS PRESS · NEW YORK

The toys in this book were invented and made by Howard E. Smith, Jr.

LIBRARY OF CONGRESS CATALOGING IN PUBLICATION DATA

Smith, Howard Everett (date)
Balance it!

SUMMARY: Suggested craft projects and activities
illustrate the principles of balance.
1. Balance—Juvenile literature. 2. Toy making—
Juvenile literature. [1. Balance. 2. Handicraft]
I. Ancona, George. II. Title.
QC107.S59   530.8   81-65907
ISBN 0-590-07608-6   AACR2

Published by Four Winds Press
A division of Scholastic Inc., New York, N.Y.
Text copyright © 1982 by Howard E. Smith, Jr.
Photographs copyright © 1982 by George Ancona
All rights reserved
Printed in the United States of America
Library of Congress Catalog Card Number: 81-65907
1   2   3   4   5   85   84   83   82

to Carroll Briggs

CONTENTS

BALANCE IT!

BALANCE

Let's Look at a Seesaw

These children are trying to balance each other on a seesaw. Since you have played on seesaws, you know why there are six small children on one side and one adult on the other. They are trying to balance their weights.

The children will move back and forth on the seesaw until it does not tilt anymore. Then they will be balanced.

You might describe balance as a feeling. Perhaps you can remember how it feels to be balanced on a seesaw.

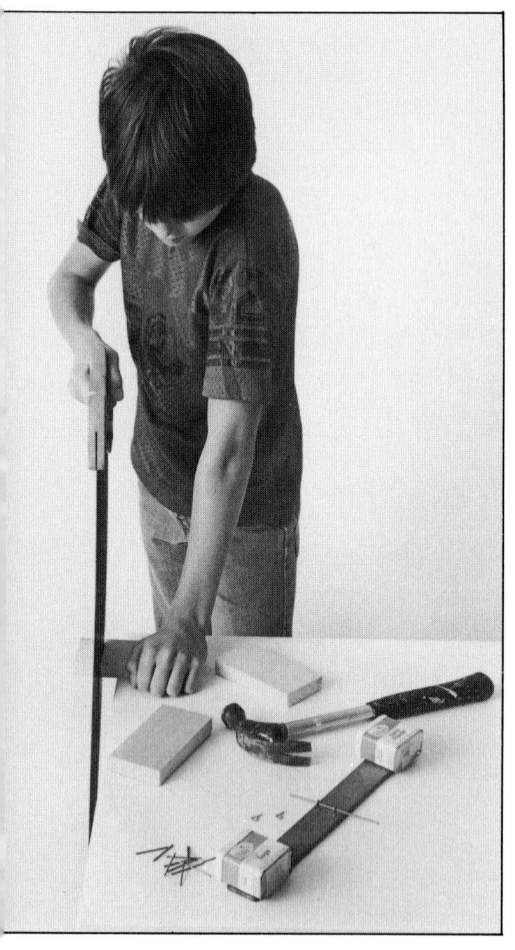

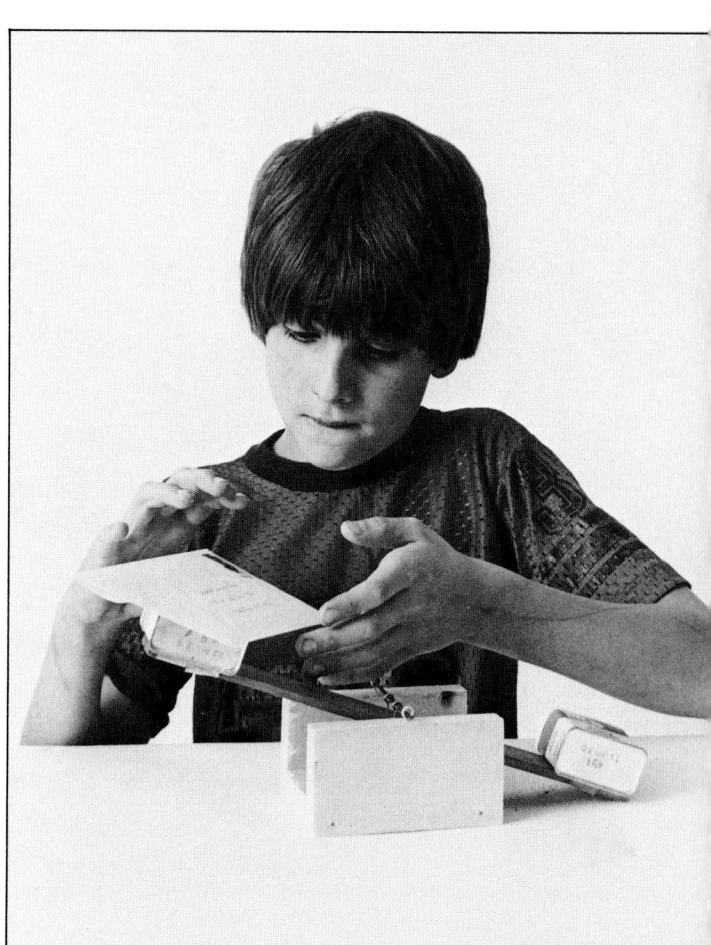

A Letter Scale

Do you like to write letters to your friends? You can easily make a scale that will show you if a letter weighs an ounce or less—or more. If your letter weighs more than an ounce, it will need more postage.

YOU WILL NEED
- one piece of wood 1 inch by 4 inches by 24 inches. (Saw this into three pieces, each 8 inches long, for the base.)
- one piece of wood ¼ inch by 2 inches by 24 inches
- four small screws with open, round ends
- stiff wire. Cut a piece from a coat hanger, using a pair of pliers.
- two full 1-ounce cans of spice. Empty one can into a small jar for use at home.
- Scotch tape to tape the cans to the board
- nails or brads 2 inches long
- saw
- hammer
- a pair of pliers

The photographs show you how to make it.

When the scale is made, place a letter on top of the empty can. If it weighs exactly one ounce, the scale will not tilt at all. If the letter weighs less than one ounce, the can with the spice in it will be lower. If the letter weighs more than one ounce, the empty can and letter will be lower.

Compare the scale with the seesaw. How are they alike? In many ways they are the same, aren't they?

A Mobile That Moves in a Breeze

Would you like to make a sculpture that moves in the slightest breeze? You can make a mobile.

YOU WILL NEED
- button thread or thin wire
- cardboard
- a dowel, ⅛ inch in diameter and approximately 4 feet long
- saw
- pencil to draw designs
- blunt-nosed scissors
- glue to stick thread or wire to the dowel
- watercolor paintbrush
- colorful nontoxic watercolors or poster paints

Saw the dowel into three pieces. Make sure that one piece is about twice the length of the other two.

From the cardboard, cut out some fish shapes or such things as hearts, stars, or snowflakes. (You may get some ideas on pages 12-13.) Tie them with threads to the shorter dowels. Put a tiny bit of glue on the threads where they touch the wood so that they do not slip.

Now tie thread around the middle of the longest dowel and hang it so that you can work easily. You will want to hang the smaller dowels on this larger one so that they balance. This means that you will have to experiment by moving your dowels back and forth, closer and farther, from the center of the long dowel.

A wonderful thing about balance is that you know when you have it. Once you are satisfied with your mobile, hang it in your room. When there is a slight draft or breeze, it will move. If your mobile has fish cutouts, they will seem to swim back and forth.

How does the mobile remind you of the seesaw and scale? The dowels are held at just one place, like the boards on the seesaw and the scale. The dowels will tilt when the weights on both sides are not in balance, just as the board does on the seesaw and the scale.

Walking with Weights

What do you do when you carry two full suitcases? You carry one in each hand. That way the weight is more evenly balanced and the suitcases are easier to carry.

What Three Dolls Can Show Us about Balance

Two dolls easily balance each other when they are placed on a third doll. If only one doll is stacked on the lower doll, both will fall over. Why? They are unbalanced.

How do the dolls remind you of the two suitcases? They are like two weights, or two suitcases, balancing each other on each side of the one doll.

To make the dolls, place a piece of tracing paper or thin tissue paper over the picture. Lightly trace the outline, then cut the shape, and pencil it onto a block of balsa wood. Balsa wood is very soft wood, and you can cut each doll with a round wood file. Make the other two dolls exactly the same way.

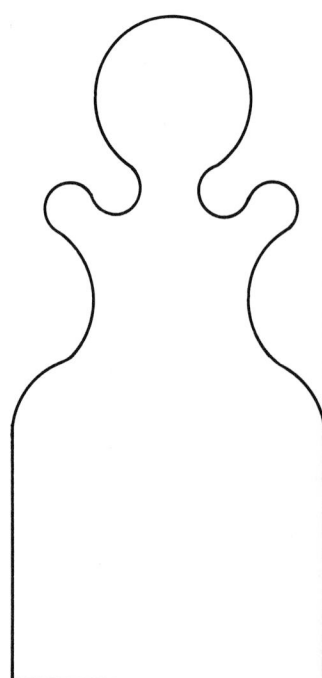

YOU WILL NEED

- tracing paper for tracing designs
- carbon paper for drawing designs onto wood
- three blocks of balsa wood 1 inch by 2 inches by 4 inches
- a round wood file, to shape the balsa wood
- nontoxic watercolors
- small, watercolor paintbrush
- plastic wood for repair jobs

Have fun stacking them. See how they balance, or fall over!

Think of other ways weight is balanced. Why do knapsacks have two shoulder straps? Why do wheelbarrows have two handles? Why do you do push-ups and chin-ups with two hands? All these things are done for balance.

SYMMETRY

Look-Alike Designs

Do you want to make some beautiful designs that are also very interesting?

YOU WILL NEED
- paper
- watercolors
- pencil
- blunt-nosed scissors
- brush

Fold a piece of paper. Using a pair of blunt scissors, cut a shape from one part of it. But, do not cut off the fold of the paper. Now open the paper. What a design!

Notice that the two halves of the paper are exactly the same size and shape.

There is a special name for such a design. Such a design is symmetrical (SIM-MEH-TRI-KAL). A design has symmetry when each half is exactly the same shape and size as the other. If you cut a symmetrical design in half, you would have two equal pieces.

Look at the girl and the window. The photograph shows us that the two sides of her body look the same. They are symmetrical. Your body is symmetrical, too.

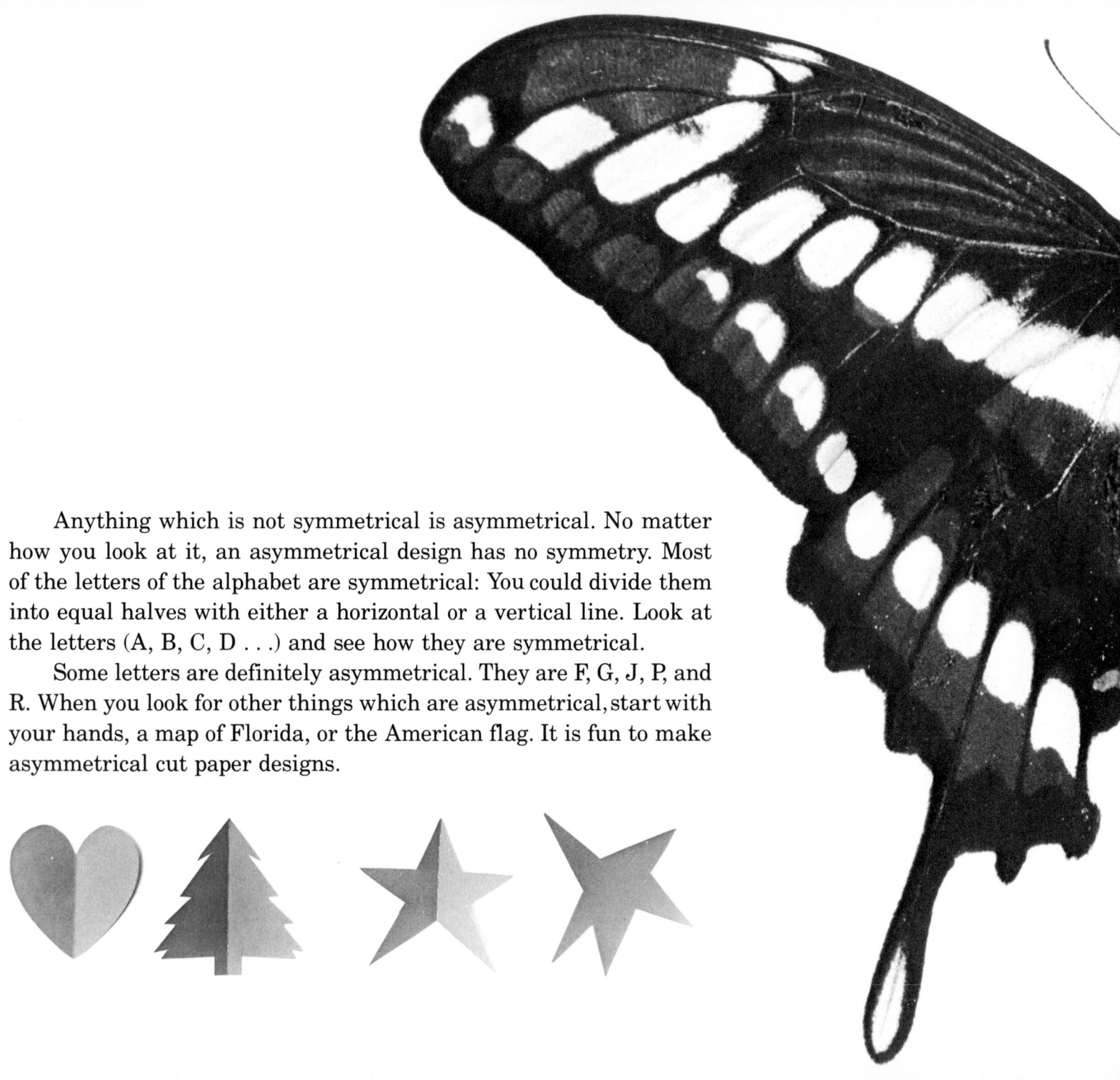

Anything which is not symmetrical is asymmetrical. No matter how you look at it, an asymmetrical design has no symmetry. Most of the letters of the alphabet are symmetrical: You could divide them into equal halves with either a horizontal or a vertical line. Look at the letters (A, B, C, D . . .) and see how they are symmetrical.

Some letters are definitely asymmetrical. They are F, G, J, P, and R. When you look for other things which are asymmetrical, start with your hands, a map of Florida, or the American flag. It is fun to make asymmetrical cut paper designs.

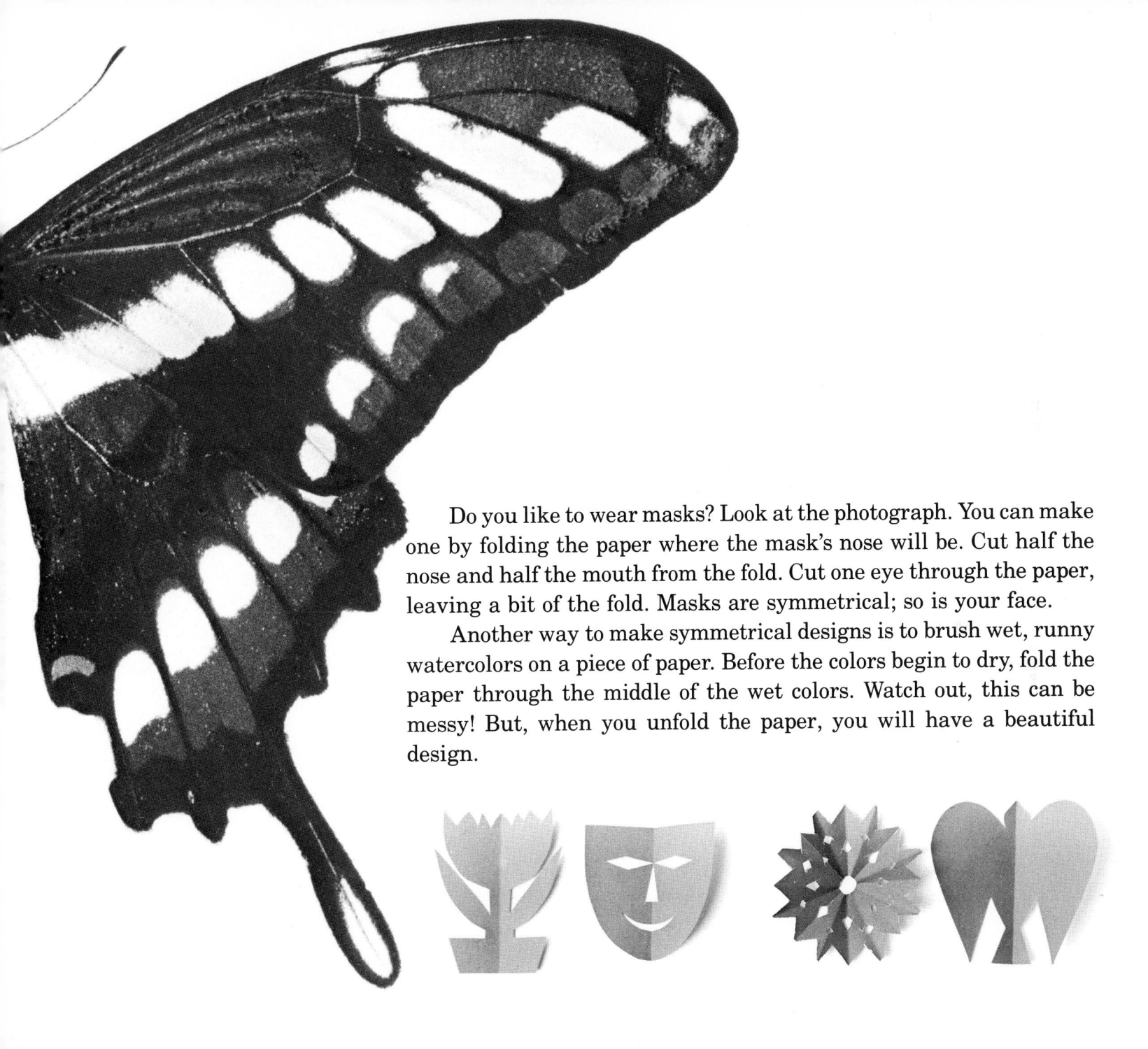

Do you like to wear masks? Look at the photograph. You can make one by folding the paper where the mask's nose will be. Cut half the nose and half the mouth from the fold. Cut one eye through the paper, leaving a bit of the fold. Masks are symmetrical; so is your face.

Another way to make symmetrical designs is to brush wet, runny watercolors on a piece of paper. Before the colors begin to dry, fold the paper through the middle of the wet colors. Watch out, this can be messy! But, when you unfold the paper, you will have a beautiful design.

A string of paper dolls has symmetry. Take a long strip of paper and fold it about two inches to the right. Make another fold under the first about two inches to the left. Then make another fold to the right ... to the left, and so on. When you get to the last fold, cut off any extra paper. Cut half of the doll design into the folded paper. Be sure to leave enough paper at the hands and feet. When you finish cutting, open it up!

Think of symmetrical shapes that please you such as buildings, vases, butterflies, and flowers. We like to see things that are balanced.

FINDING THE CENTER OF GRAVITY

All objects are pulled downward to the earth by a force known as gravity.

Have you ever balanced a Frisbee on one finger? If you have, you already know how to find the Frisbee's center of gravity because *the center of gravity is the place around which an object balances.*

Everything has a center of gravity. Can you balance these on your finger: a foot ruler, a jar lid, a square piece of cardboard? You will find the center of gravity at the center of these objects.

Tennis balls, basketballs, and Ping-Pong balls are round objects. Each one has a center of gravity in its center. The earth is a round object, too, with a center of gravity. This center of gravity is right in the center of the earth.

A Plumb Bob

You can use this knowledge in many ways. Builders often use a plumb bob to see if the sides of a building are straight up and down.

YOU WILL NEED
• a weight
• a string

A plumb bob is simply a weight on a string.

The gravity of the earth pulls the weight on the end of this string, and the string itself, in a straight line, points toward the center of the earth.

17

18

An Easy-to-Make Balancing Sculpture

Would you like to make a sculpture that will look as if it is floating on air?

YOU WILL NEED
- cardboard, such as the side of a corrugated cardboard box
- heavy, stiff paper
- thread
- a weight, such as a heavy washer
- thumbtacks
- blunt-nosed scissors
- pencil
- compass to make a circle

Draw an oddly shaped design on a piece of cardboard. Cut it out.

You can find the center of gravity in this asymmetrical piece of cardboard by using a plumb bob. Hold the string, as shown in the photograph, anyplace on the edge of the cardboard. Let the weight hang free. Be sure not to hold the cardboard too tightly. Let it swing freely between your fingers.

The string will pass right through the center of gravity of the cardboard, because the weight is pulled straight downward by the earth's center of gravity.

With your pencil, mark the string line. Someplace on that line is the cardboard's center of gravity. Repeat this, holding the plumb bob at two different places on the cardboard. You will end up with three marks on the cardboard. They will cross at one point. Where they cross is the place which marks the center of gravity.

Once this boy found the center of gravity of his piece of cardboard, he made an interesting sculpture. You can, too.

The cone he uses is made of stiff paper. To make a cone, use the compass to make a wide circle. Cut out the circle, then cut one straight line from the edge to the center. Twist the paper inward, tape it, and you will have a cone.

Because the center of gravity is the place around which an object balances, you will be able to place your sculpture so that it will seem to float in the air. It stays level and does not tilt. It is balanced.

YOUR CENTER OF GRAVITY

All living things—such as birds, cows, and humans—have centers of gravity. The most interesting center of gravity, for you, is your own. Oddly, your center of gravity is not always in one place. It can, and does, move. Whenever you move your head, legs, or arms, your center of gravity moves.

If you take yoga, gymnastics, or dance class, you may hear the teacher refer to your "center." This is your center of gravity, and you must balance around it.

With your feet together and your arms at your sides, your center of gravity is someplace in the middle of your body. Can you imagine it? It is purely imaginary: It is not real as your liver, kidneys, and brain are real. Yet, if you can imagine where it is, knowing about your center of gravity will help you to balance.

Stand straight with both legs and arms together. Put your right leg as far as you can to the right. Can you stay balanced? Did you shoot your arm out in another direction so you wouldn't fall? Or did you lean back? Probably. Why? Your center of gravity has shifted to the right, so you immediately try to balance yourself by putting your arm in another direction. As you get better at balancing, you will start to be able to control the way the weight moves around your center of gravity.

You move by moving your center of gravity. Try shifting your center of gravity in a swimming pool. While floating, stick out an arm or a leg. Feel how easily you roll over in the water.

You must shift your center of gravity many, many times a day. You do it, for example, every time you walk. When you walk, you put one leg forward at a time. Your center of gravity moves forward. You become unbalanced and fall forward toward your foot. You put your weight on your forward foot and, for a moment, become balanced. Then you move the other leg, and your center of gravity moves again. As you walk, you keep becoming balanced and unbalanced. Your center of gravity keeps shifting.

Odd as it may seem, you can get into a position where your center of gravity is actually outside your body. Stand on your hands and legs with your knees and elbows straight. Put your head down between your arms. Where is your center of gravity now? It's a few inches under your chest. Everything balances around the center of gravity.

RAISING THE CENTER OF GRAVITY

Stilts and Unicycles

Get some blocks and make a stack of them. As the stack gets higher, the center of gravity is raised. As the center of gravity is raised, the stack starts to wobble. It becomes unbalanced and the blocks fall over.

When the center of gravity is raised in an object, the object becomes less stable. An object with a high center of gravity will fall over more easily than an object with a low center of gravity. In other words, as the center of gravity in an object is raised *up*, the object can more easily fall *down*.

Look at one boy enjoying his unicycle and the other enjoying his stilts. It takes time to learn how to balance on stilts and unicycles because it is more difficult to be balanced with a high center of gravity. But what fun!

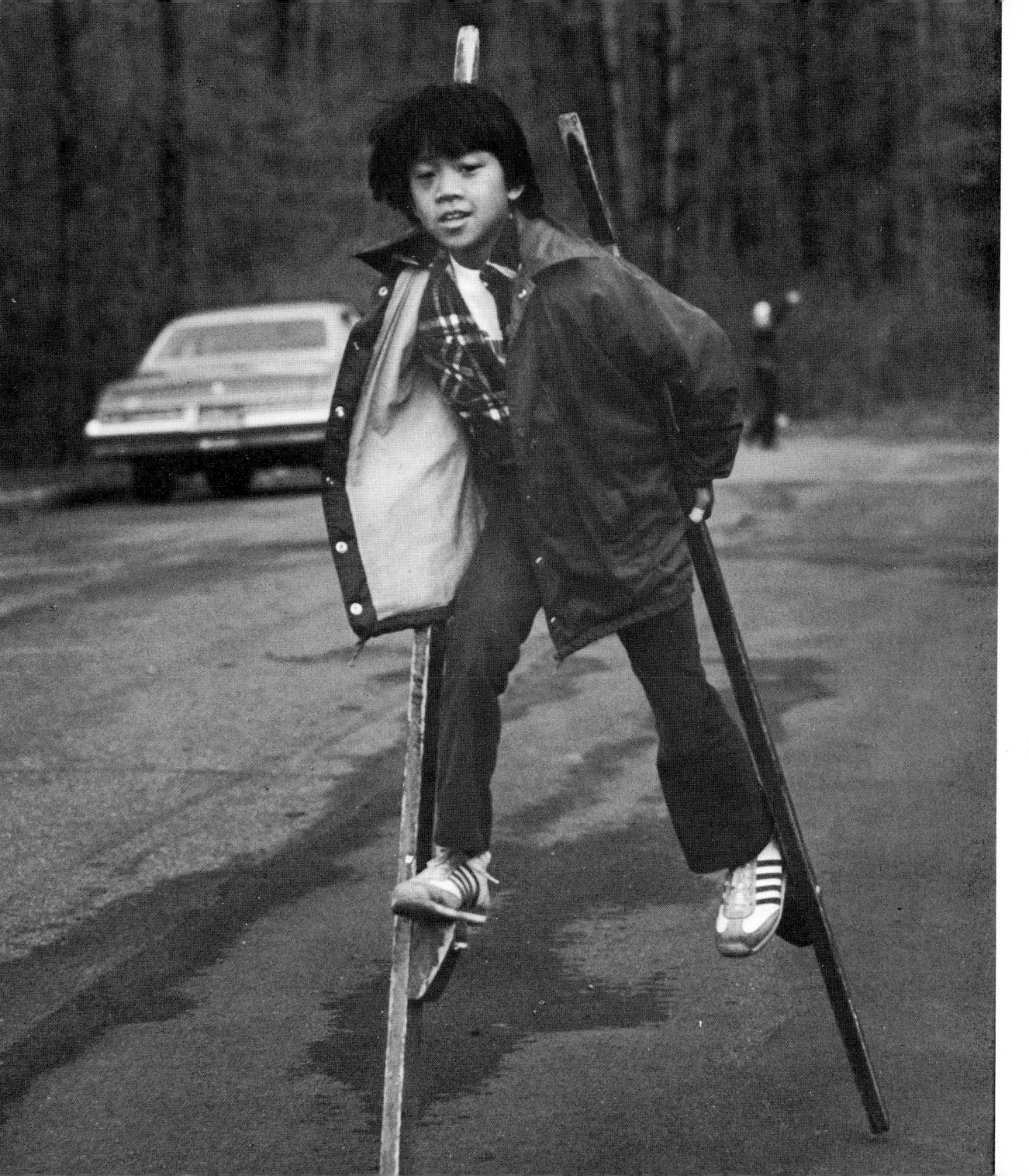

LOWERING THE CENTER OF GRAVITY

A Balancing Doll

Just as it is more difficult to be balanced with a high center of gravity, it is easier to be balanced with a low center of gravity.

Here is a balancing doll. She is on top of a soda bottle. Do you think she'll fall over? Guess again. If you tip her, she will stand right up. You can't keep her down.

Why does she always come back up? What is the trick? The weights on the long wires (her arms) are the secret. They are heavier than the balancing doll itself. They keep the center of gravity low. When the center of gravity in an object is as low as possible, the object cannot fall down anymore. You could say it has fallen as far as it can fall. This is why when the center of gravity is low, it helps to keep things balanced.

You can easily have a balancing doll of your own.

YOU WILL NEED
- a block of balsa wood 1 inch by 2 inches by 4 inches.
  (You can use a larger block if you want to.)
- heavy washers
- two equal lengths of stiff wire
- nontoxic watercolors
- paintbrush
- thread to tie the washers to the wire
- glue to stick the thread onto the washers and wire
- plastic wood for repairs, if needed
- a round wood file

Trace the drawing onto a block of balsa wood. Shape it into the figure of a doll with a file. Paint your doll and when it dries, push two wires into the sides, for arms. If they are loose, make them secure with plastic wood or glue. The weights are heavy washers. Tie them to the wires with thread. Glue the threads so that they will hold.

Place the doll on a bottle and give her a push. Watch how she balances herself.

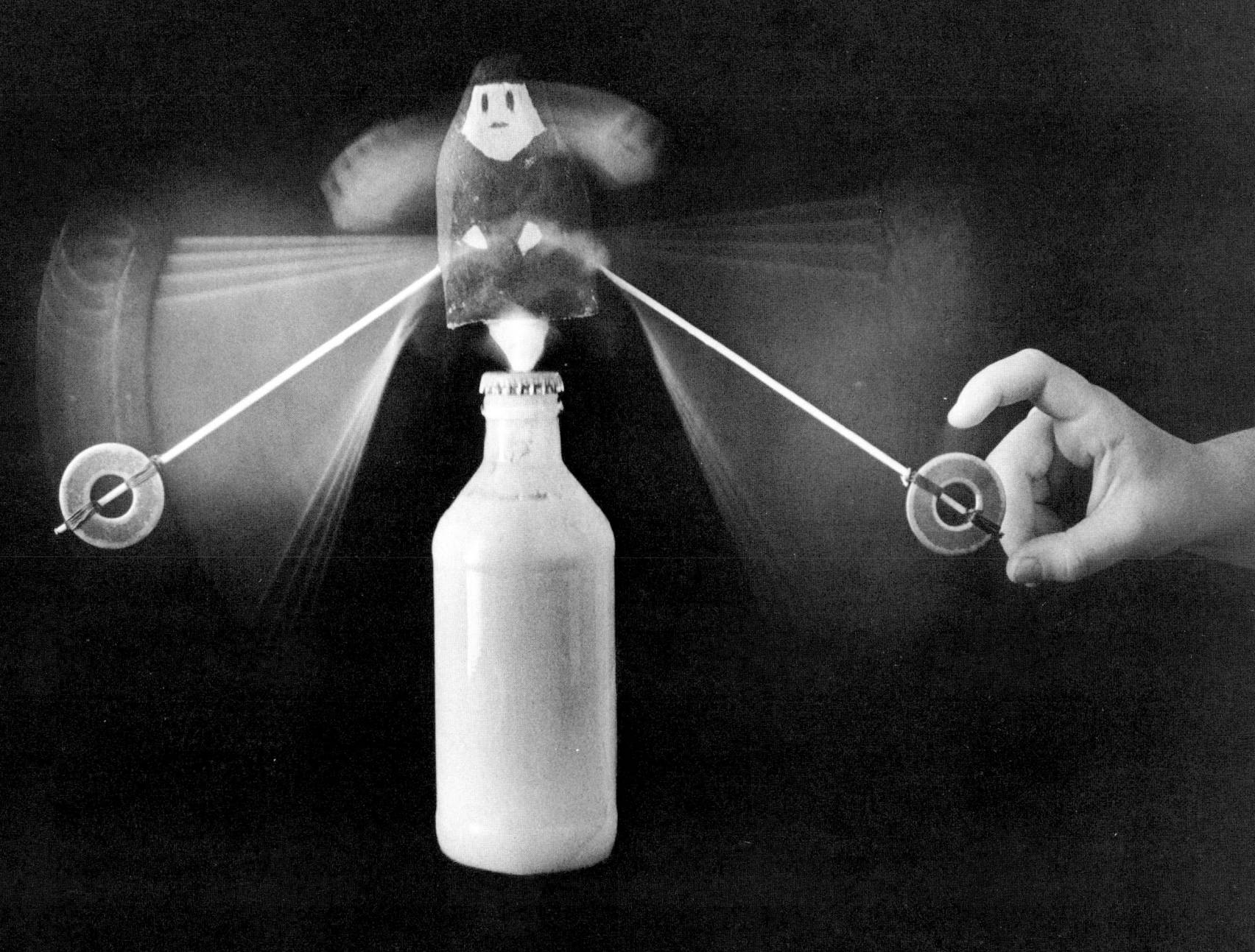

On a Balance Beam

Look at the boy on the balance beam. He is steadying himself with a long pole, which has weights attached to it. How does he remind you of the balancing doll? The weights help the boy balance, by lowering his center of gravity.

Sailboats

Have you ever watched sailboats move in the wind? Have you ever wondered why they did not tip over, especially when the wind pushed against their sails?

Keels keep sailboats from tipping over. Keels are the lowest parts of a boat. They stick deep down in the water. Most of the time they are made of heavy metal. See the photograph of a keel. Next time you are by the sea or a large lake, go to a boatyard and look at the keels on sailboats.

Because keels are heavy and deep in the water, they lower the center of gravity of a boat. When a sailboat rolls on the waves, the keel makes it roll back easily so that it will stay upright. Do you remember how the balancing doll did that?

A keel also helps the sailboat when the wind pushes on the sails. When the wind blows on the sails, a sailboat sometimes leans way over. If there were no keel, the wind would push the boat all the way over.

You can easily understand how a keel works. Get a solid rubber ball, which can float. Put a long heavy nail in it, so that most of the nail is sticking out of the ball.

Put the ball into a bathtub of water. Make waves. Try to tip the ball over. Perhaps you can tip it over, but the ball will quickly roll back in the water so that the nail (which is like a keel) will always be down. This will give you an idea of how a keel works.

Kite Flying

As you look at the kite, keep in mind the keel and balancing doll. The kite has a long tail made of colorful rags. The extra weight of the tail is actually heavier than the kite itself. It gives the kite a low center of gravity.

Why would you want your kite to have a low center of gravity? If there is no tail on a kite, it will turn over and over in the wind. When that happens, the kite usually crashes. When the center of gravity is low, the kite flies more steadily. The weight of the tail keeps the kite from turning upside down. Next time you fly a kite test different tails. Have some short, others long and see what happens.

MOVING THE CENTER OF GRAVITY FROM SIDE TO SIDE

Have you ever been on a swing which was so high that your feet did not touch the ground? Do you remember how you worked to get the swing moving?

You first had to put your legs out in front of you. When you did that, you moved your center of gravity forward. That unbalanced the swing. It too moved forward. To go backward you brought your legs under you. That unbalanced the swing. It moved backward.

By putting your legs out and bringing them back many times you got your swing moving, going higher and higher, faster and faster.

A swing only moves when it is unbalanced. By making it unbalanced, over and over again, you can keep one moving.

A swing is a type of pendulum. Anything that swings back and forth—like a swing—is a pendulum. It will go back and forth in even movements. The plumb bob you made on page 17 would become a pendulum if it were hung someplace so that it could move freely.

The Pendulum Picture Maker

Do you want to make unusual pictures with a pendulum picture maker? You can.

The pendulum picture maker is a little more difficult than other projects in this book, but it is not as hard as it looks. Once you know how to make a pendulum picture maker you can make wonderful pictures with your friends. If your school has a fair or a carnival to raise money, this project can be part of an attractive booth.

YOU WILL NEED
- a place where you can hang a plumb bob
- a table
- wire or heavy, strong string which is able to hold fifty pounds or more
- a heavy weight, such as a window-sash weight or pail of sand or dirt
- one board about 1 inch by 6 inches by 12 inches
- a dowel, ¼ inch in diameter and about 4 feet long. Saw into pieces.
- small screws ⅛ inch wide. You use them to make holes through the dowels. Easy does it!
- two 1-inch-long nails, also called twopenny common nails
- several sheets of acetate, at least 10 inches by 14 inches in size, or some other very slick paper
- one large C clamp
- a free-flowing felt-tip pen
- rubber bands to hold the pen to the dowel
- pliers to bend nails
- hammer
- a small saw, such as a jigsaw
- a small screwdriver

Saw the dowel into two pieces, one about twice as long as the other.

Prepare the dowels by tapping holes into them first, with a thin nail, at the places they will join. Make the holes larger by putting screws in them. Easy! Refer to the photograph, and you will see that you need to connect the smaller dowel to the board on the table and to the larger dowel. You need to connect the larger dowel to the pendulum (which you have made by fastening a heavy weight on a wire to a beam) and to the smaller dowel.

This must be done so that the pieces of dowel can move freely, so make your nail holes big, then fasten the pieces together with bent nails.

Attach the pen to the long dowel with rubber bands.

To make a design, pull the pendulum back. Release it and let it swing. As long as the pendulum is unbalanced it will swing. When it is balanced it will stop. By then you will have an interesting picture. It will show the trail left by the unbalanced pendulum as it moved.

Pull the pendulum in different directions, for different designs.

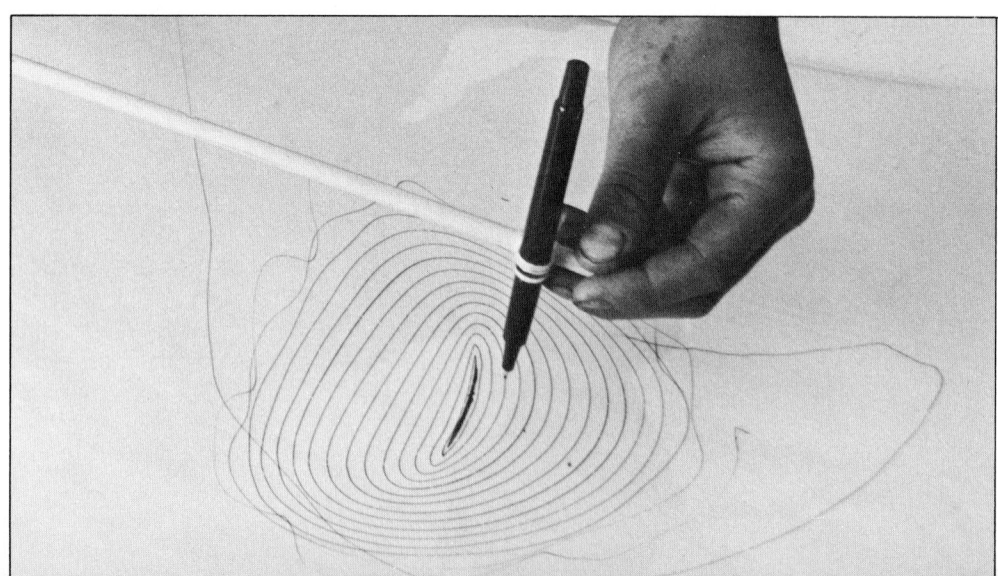

Paper Airplanes

You can have fun experimenting with a paper airplane. You will also find out why airplanes must be balanced.

YOU WILL NEED
- heavy bond paper or other stiff, heavy paper, to make a model plane
- small paper clips
- blunt-nosed scissors

Balance your plane with paper clips. First, put a paper clip behind the wing and try to fly the airplane. It probably will not fly at all.

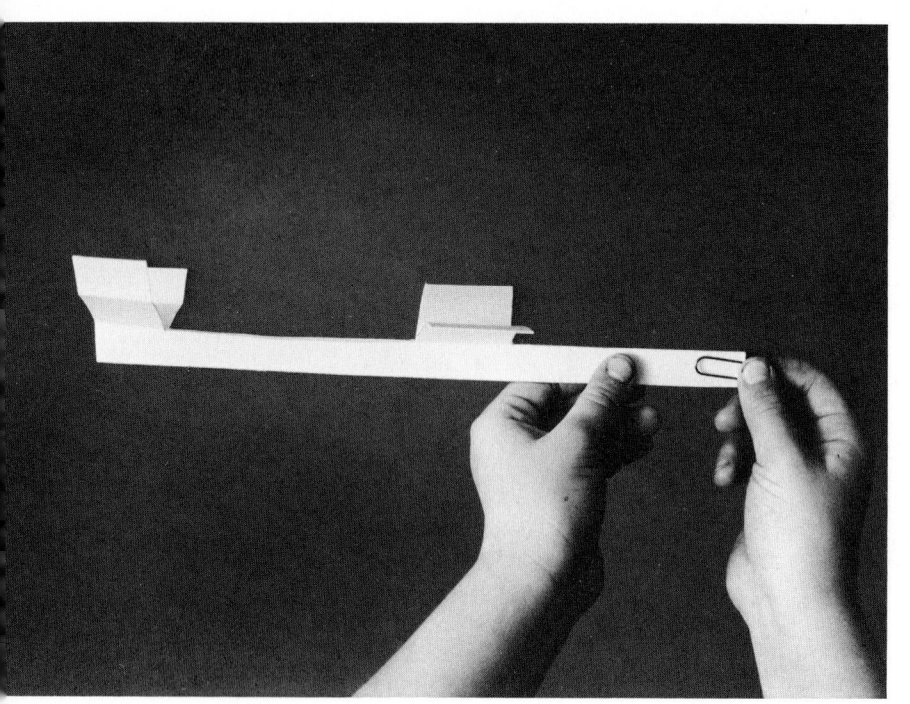

Next, fly the airplane with the paper clip near its nose. It will fly much better. Shift the paper clip back and forth until the airplane flies as well as it can. You may have to add more paper clips.

Try placing a paper clip on one wing. What happens? The airplane will swerve toward the side with the paper clip.

How often you shift the weight of your body without thinking about it! How do you turn your bicycle or switch direction on your sled? You shift your center of gravity by moving your weight from side to side.

YOU AND BALANCE

The feeling of balance is a very important feeling. You have been developing yours since before you were born. You have a "sense of balance," and it is a sense but balance isn't one of the five senses. Those are hearing, smelling, tasting, touching, and seeing.

How do you sense balance? Tubes inside of your ears help. There are three tubes. They are called semicircular canals. Each one has liquid inside of it. Every time you move in any direction, the liquid also moves. Special nerves inside of the tubes feel the moving liquid and they send messages about it to your brain. These messages tell you about how your head and body have moved. When you get these messages, you move muscles in your body so that you can be balanced.

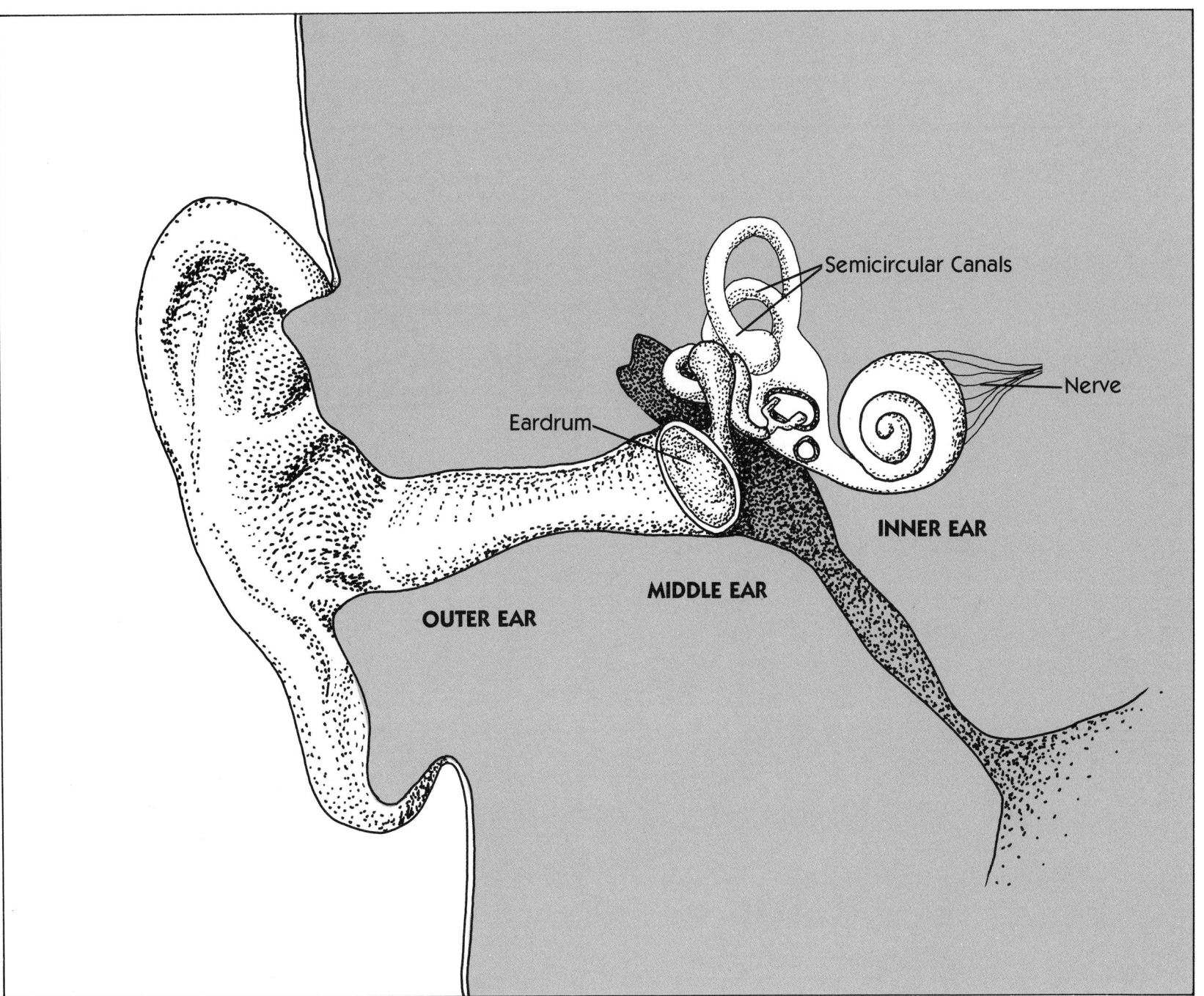

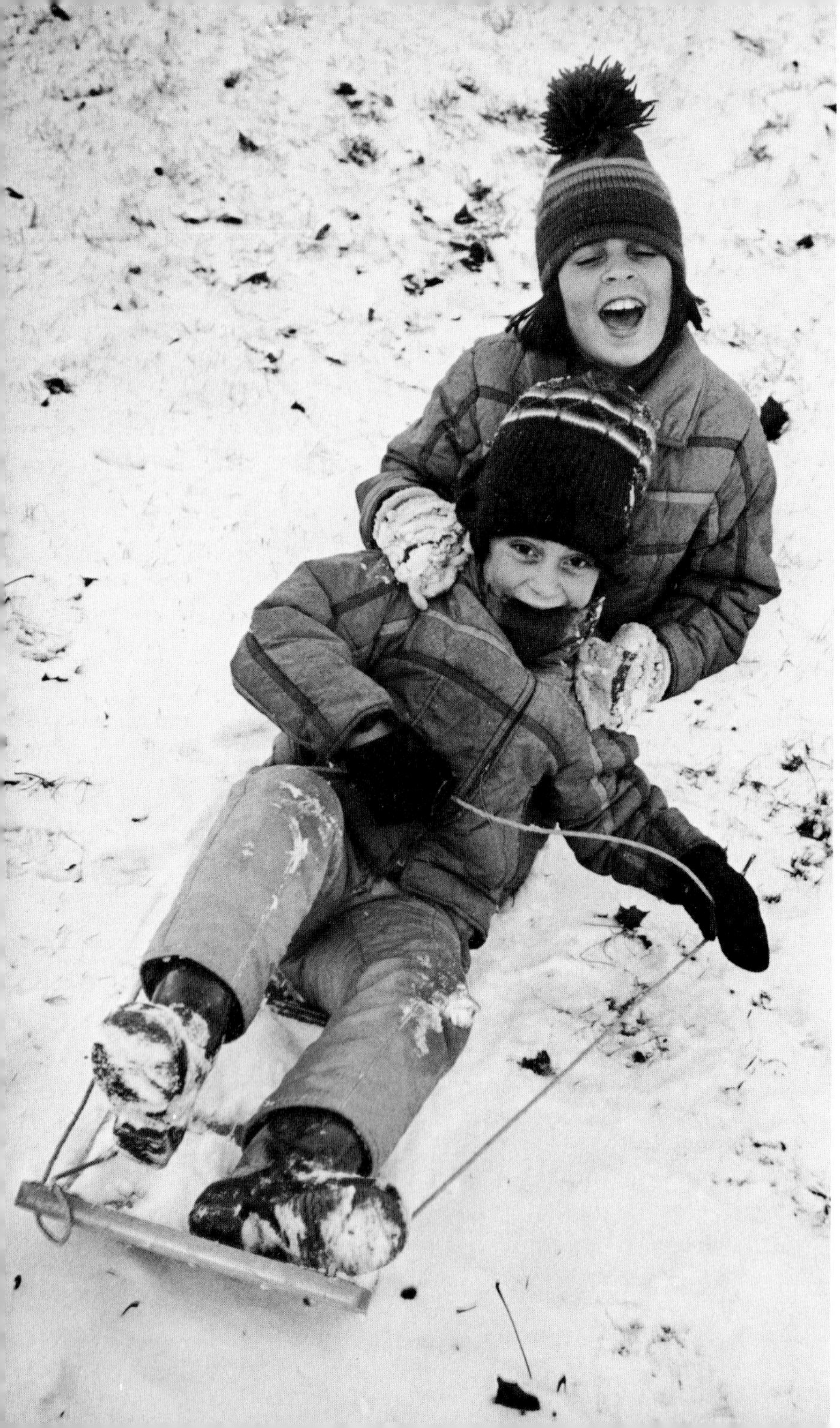
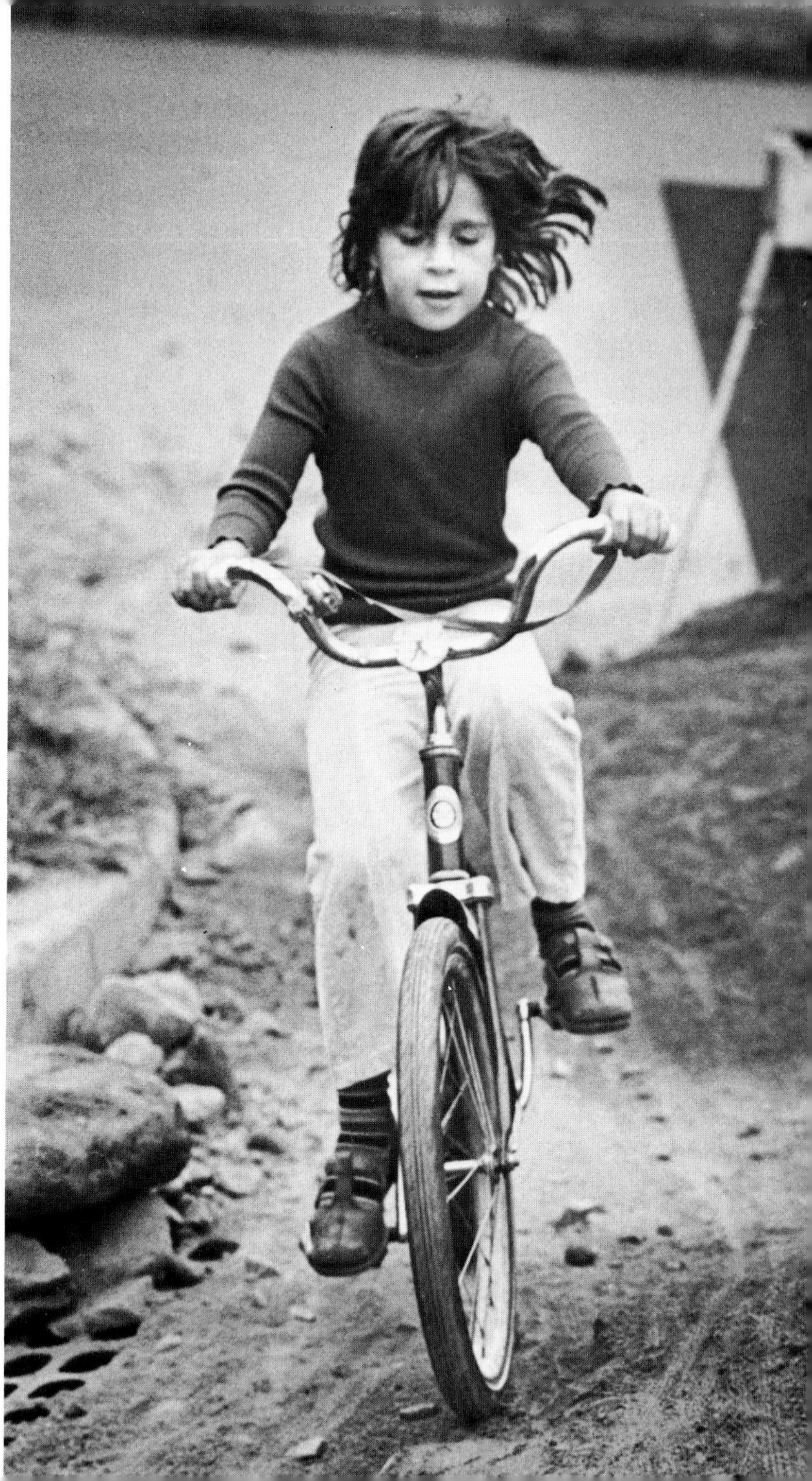

Your sense of balance gives you many different feelings. It gives you a thrilling feeling when you race downhill on a sled or dive from a high board through the air or turn over in a somersault. It gives you a dizzy feeling, if you spin round and round. You can feel seasick on a boat when your sense of balance is upset.

But, most of the time, your sense of balance makes you feel good. It almost seems to work automatically. But by concentrating on that feeling of balance and remembering ways you adjust your body, you can become even more skilled at many of the things you enjoy.